First Published in the United States of America in 2009
First edition

Gingko Press, Inc.

1321 Fifth Street
Berkeley, CA 94710, USA

Phone (510) 898-1195

Fax (510) 898-1196
email: books@gingkopress.com

www.gingkopress.com

ISBN: 978-1-58423-361-9

Printed in China

© 2009 JUXTAPOZ
www.juxtapoz.com

Edited by: M. Revelli
Project Management: Saelee Oh
Writer: Evan Pricco
Special Thanks: Ellen Christensen, Ely Kim, Joel Speasmaker, Gwynn Vitello, Diana Weber

Additional Credits: Bryce Ward for Dennis McNett's parade photos
(bryceward.com) and The Breeder, Athens for Stelios Faitakis' images and Errikos Arones
Collection, Alexander McQueen Collection and Collection of Themistocles and Dare Michos for
Stelios Faitakis' collector credits.

Previous Page Image by: Jeff Soto
Opposite Page Image by: Polly Morgan

Cover Image by: Marci Washington

CONTENTS

INTRODUCTION

Juxtapoz Art & Culture Magazine

Juxtapoz Dark Arts beguiles with visions of demons, black magic, witchcraft, and the abnormal. A carnival of subject matter ranges from mythical monsters, ghosts, black humor, and lonely characters to gruesome scenes of death and destruction. Upon closer view, deeper meanings and metaphors are discovered within often disturbing and despondent scenes. Ultimately, *Dark Arts* celebrates beauty in the macabre, revitalizing a long history of Romanticism - as Victor Hugo penned, "As a means of contrast with the sublime, the grotesque is, in our view, the richest source that nature can offer."

Scaremongers have always predicted that troubled times are upon us, but in the 21st century, these troubles are broadcast on 24-hour television channels, news tickers on the sides of buildings, blogs, and Internet search engines. We are bombarded by distress every day. Although some catastrophes are real, modern society struggles with ubiquitous mania. However, oversaturation and manipulation by the media are being subverted and contested by a diverse group of talented contemporary artists.

The artists in this collection employ unique ways to express the subject matter. Some use humorous and disturbing imagery, while others employ bittersweet and melancholic symbolism. One artist may use monsters, ghosts, beasts, and zombies in a piece, while another takes human characters and isolates personal demons through metaphorical darkness. Human nature and a critical look at society are the common themes. And of course there is death - not necessarily in plain view, but ever looming.

The *Dark Arts* artists can hardly be pigeonholed as doomsayers. Juxtapoz has always championed hope and the power to seek change through creativity. The imagery may represent death or darkness, but there is something life affirming in the emotion. Throughout *Dark Arts* is a celebration of expression and beauty that triumphs despite the intense pressures of modernity, allowing societal and personal imperfections to shine through.

Image by: Herbert Baglione

Herbert Baglione

As far as my career, nothing in this world is so solid that it can't turn to dust. That's what I believe. If the work is really good it overcomes time and barriers. What's been important to me is feeling alive in what I'm doing. I seek to develop good work. What's really changed is that I have had a certain time to breathe and to see where I come from; to feel the wind on my face again is something priceless.

To me, the act of painting is a religious process; the fact of being very focused, sometimes in silence, translates as a ritual, and it's possible to notice whether or not the artist is present through the work. A lot of critics say that painting has definitely died because of the market. But the truth is that painting occupies a role for which photography will never be a substitute, as video will not replace photography. I believe that a lot of paintings are able to move theviewer to look at life differently.

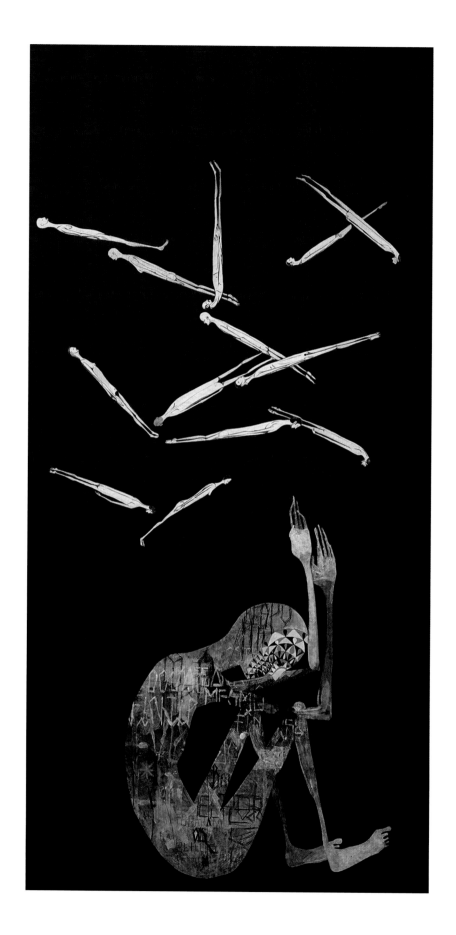

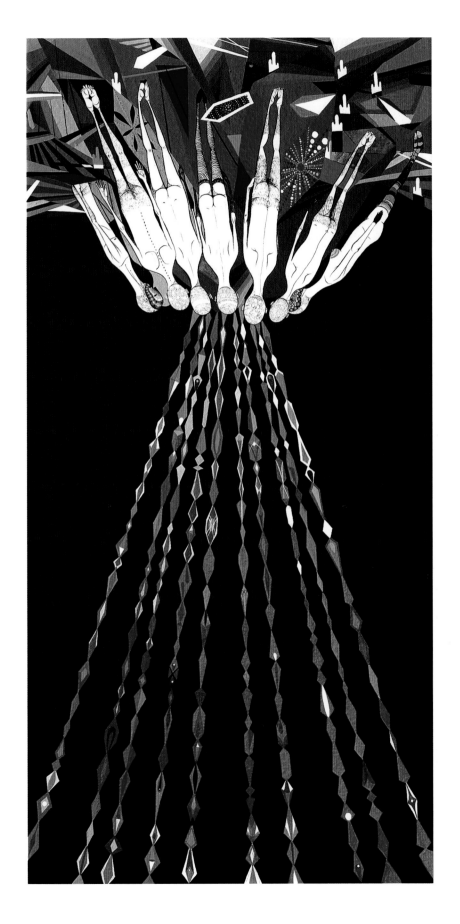

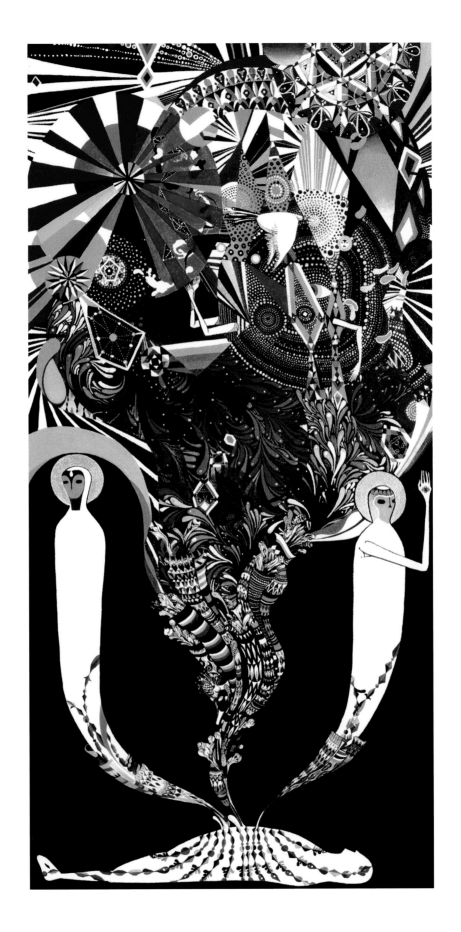

Wendy Cogan-Toyoda

My work is about an obsession with overabundance. It is the idea that one can make themselves so satisfied with what they consume, they could not possibly desire anything more. We confuse abundance with quality in the search for self-satisfaction. I align symbols of the decorative with the cheap, gaudy and luxurious to create an atmosphere of discomfort. The work can be seen as being dark or creepy, but really it is the combination of the ugly and the beautiful that generates this surreal and uneasy sense. I want to elevate the status of the ugly and create it into something that is desirable. I want to raise the question of what it is to be feminine. We all wish to attain beauty, but often find that this goal leads to vanity and over-consumption. Contrasting imagery flips our preconceptions of what is aesthetic and what it means to be attractive.

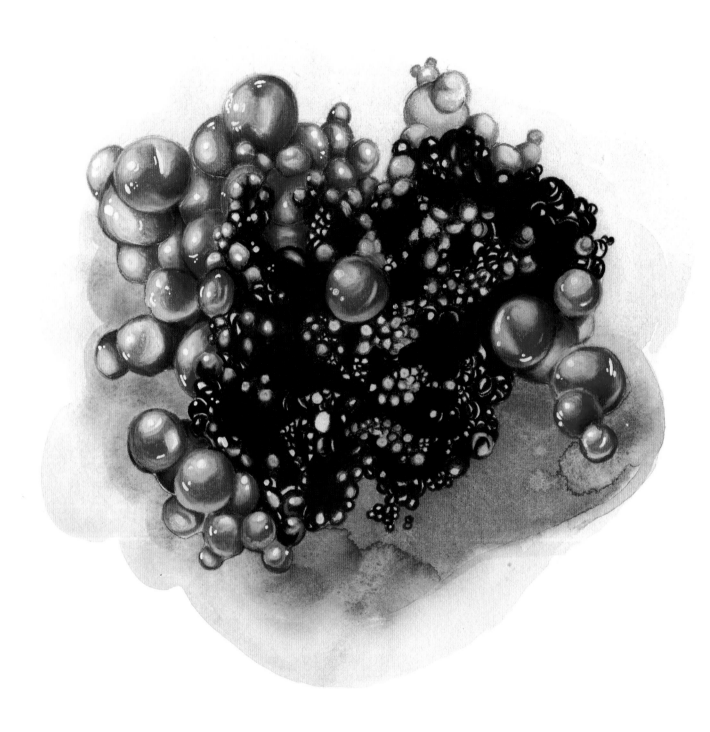

Richard Colman

Richard Colman cuts a strange and surreal incision revealing an unfiltered world. The horror vacui's claustrophobic fear of emptiness and the black holes' endless perspectives become one whilst the obsessive repetition becomes a relief from the meaningless logic of everyday life, as well as a trap, incarcerating impulse.

Colman's characteristic symbolic naked men, faceless bears, women dressed in black and baroque skeleton heads inhabit worlds where the infinite spectre of the rainbow becomes an unfathomable red thread. A thread that confuses and at the same time creates coherence while it turns familiar tunes upside down. Contrasts and similarities explode in colourful cascades, flooding definite truths. Colman's work assaults the viewer with the madness of the world, but also expands the horizon for man's eternal attempt to find his or her own unique trait in the world - whether in life, love, art, etc

-Nanna Thylstrup

DARK ARTS | 31

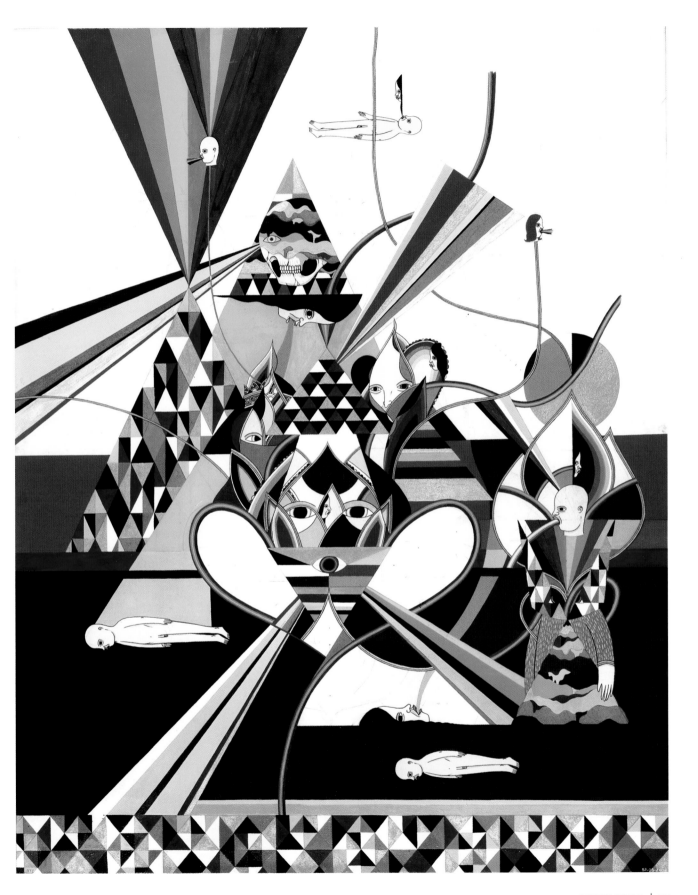

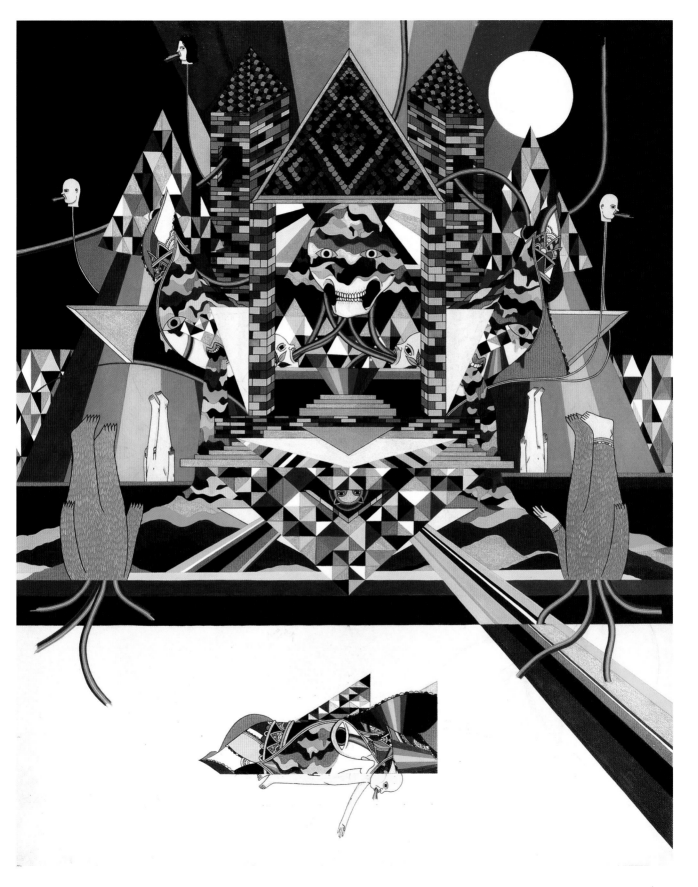

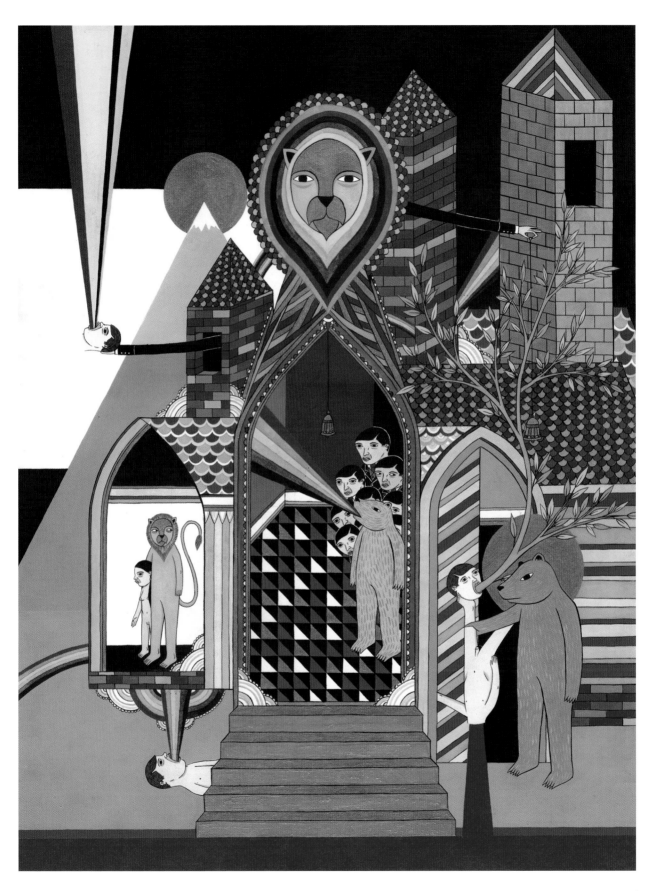

Irana Douer

That which is different calls my attention. I'm always looking for the ugliness in beauty and the beauty in the ugliness, and I try to include these flaws in my work. I like to create sinister, strange, and mysterious looking people who seem to be keeping a really good secret inside of them. Magic, energy and strange behaviours are always disturbing yet amazing.

My work is about women as independent universes, embracing their bodies and the true powers that control them. Inside their universe everything is related. Within it, surges a place from which they can acknowledge, learn, and control their own feelings and spirits.

I freely use many kinds of symbols and combine them in different ways to create a personal cosmos. I like people to interpret these symbols in their own way and am interested in generating images that are shocking but dreamy at the same time and allude to the imagination.

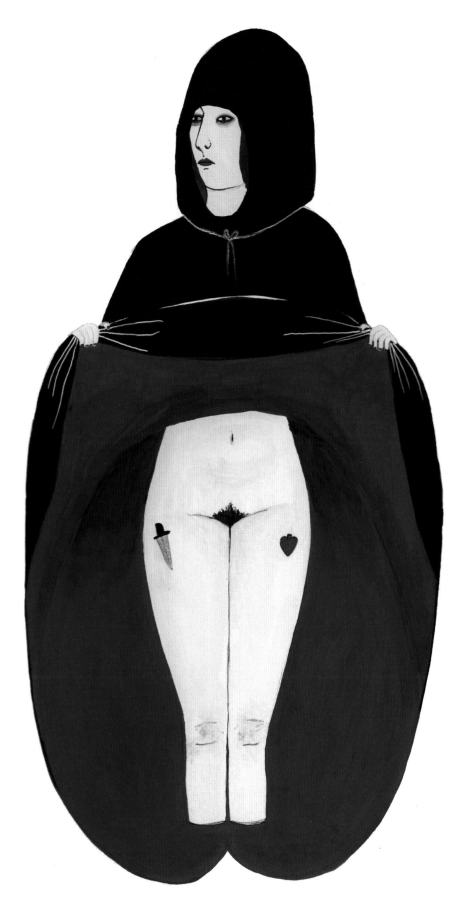

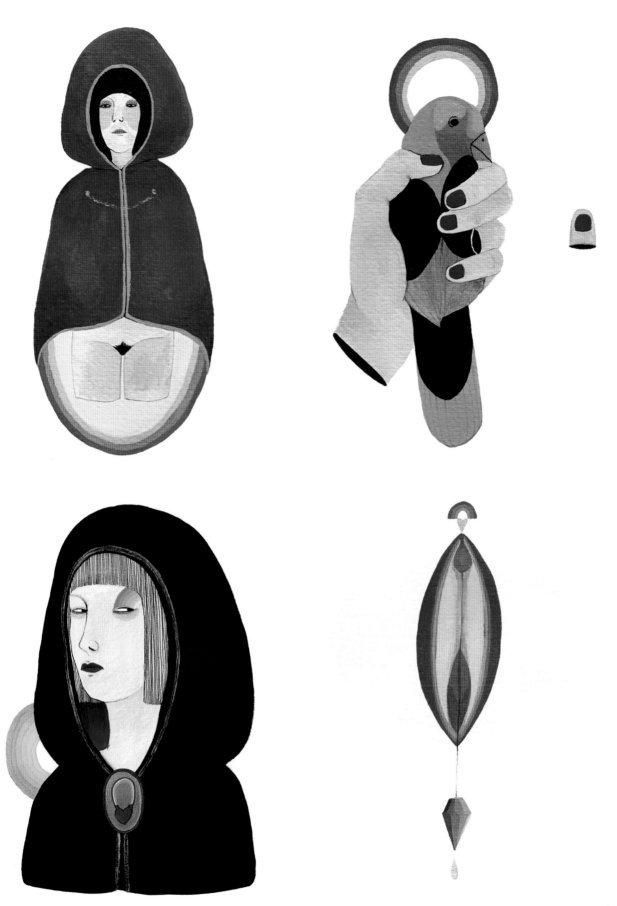

Stelios Faitakis

My pictures are about the human being, the human condition, the question of God, existence and our relationship to our surroundings. I am still trying to keep it on that general and most basic level as I feel that humanity hasn't morally progressed much after many centuries of philosophy and scientific research. On the contrary, we have found ways to justify the domination of our worst qualities over the positive ones and as a result, we got ourselves to where we are today. For me, this is not a very flattering picture, but we are still potentially capable of doing the best. Unfortunately I do not see any positive change in the near future, and what I actually think is that we are going straight to hell all together. The ways out of this have been known for many years now, but not applied. Strange creatures we are...

Matt Furie

I have always had an interest in the dark arts. As a kid, my favorite things to draw were monsters, dragons and medieval weapons. I remember going to the library in search of illustrated books on weapons and torture equipment. My favorite weapon was the crossbow (or maybe the double bladed axe) and my favorite piece of torture equipment was the iron maiden. I liked the iron maiden for aesthetic reasons, not because I liked the idea of someone going inside and getting stabbed with a million spikes and opening the thing up and seeing a bloody mess that was once a person. I played video games like "Golden Axe" and "Altered Beast" and "Shadow of the Beast" and remember really being inspired to draw creatures and characters after playing these kinds of games. There is just something about the right looking skull or a heavy metal monster face. Something about certain dark and cartoonish images have a special place in my heart. I'm about to turn 30 and I'm still drawing creatures with fur, fangs and claws because it's awesome.

Seonna Hong

I hold my cards pretty close to my chest. I'm an open book to those who know me well, but even then I'm extremely protective and sensitive to vulnerabilities, secrets and lies... whether they be my own or others'. But these thoughts that throb and throw long shadows across my mind inevitably find their way to my work.

My paintings have taken a very personal turn in the last few years. They are, in a way, like journal pages... sometimes because it's difficult to find the words... sometimes because my feelings about an experience are too overwhelming or too abstract to write down so I hide meaning in deeply coded narrative scenes... and a lot of times, and this may be a remnant from the time my mother read my diary when I was 16, it's simply because I fear incrimination.

I'm so grateful to have this outlet.

James Jean

Persephone stumbles through Hades with her pomegranate-flavored dogs.

In this blind excavation of the landscape, she will encounter fields of scholar's rocks, writhing swans, and cleft-headed peach boys playing hide and seek in the shadows.

Meanwhile, the willow tree oozes its last remaining sap, teased out into a golden rope by four thirsty finches.

The rope will help guide her through the circular labyrinth - the thought of reaching the maze's end causes her floral circulatory system to flush with pollen, leaving her breathless.

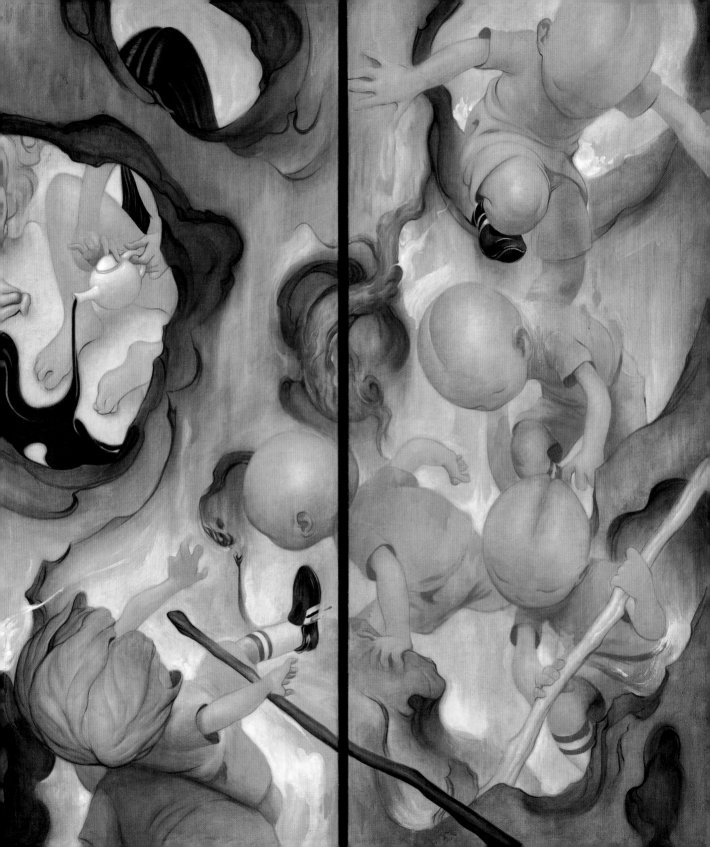

Travis Louie

I'm not so sure I stay connected to my youth through my paintings or that they keep me "forever young," but I do like to try and capture the feeling of wonder I got when I was a boy watching those atomic age sci-fi and horror films. If anything, the act of painting keeps me grounded and maybe has a kind of Rip Van Winkle effect. Time seems to stop when I'm working on my pieces. I feel like I should always try and have a healthy, almost playful enthusiasm about making my paintings and I hope some of that translates to the people viewing the work at exhibitions.

Chris Mars

My figures are real in that they express my feelings about things that exist in reality - prejudice, persecution, pain and relief. My intent is to present a mood that can be taken at first glance to be disturbing or strange, exemplifying this: Human beings, innately visual creatures, have a tendency to respond abruptly to how things might appear or look. Observing how people responded to my brother's schizophrenia, I learned that it is too easy for people to stigmatize or misjudge out of fear and misunderstanding. This extends to how people may become bigoted - socially, religiously, and ethnically. In the end, how people behave toward one another is far more horrifying than any work of art. Though my paintings have been described as nightmarish, I don't personally feel this way, or consider them dark. Instead I am hopeful that they are a conduit to start or continue a conversation based on these themes.

Elizabeth McGrath

At midnight on my 13th birthday, I did acid for the first (and last) time. We didn't really know what it was. My friend stole it from his older brother and it just looked like a tiny piece of paper. The next day, my parents said they were going to take me to the Wild Animal Park, but instead they took me to a Baptist girls' home where a fat lady sat on me for almost an hour and an old biker man, Brother Palmer, told me I was possessed by the Devil. They carried me into the closet-sized 'Get Right with God' room and played religious tapes outside my door. When I was first in the room, I tried to talk to Satan. I figured since they were so into God, maybe Satan might be real too. If I was possessed by him, maybe I could channel his energy to start fires, have super human strength, or a legion of demons could bust me out of there. Plus, I think I was still feeling the effects of the acid. After being in there for almost three months, I gave up on Satan, became a Christian and they let me out of the room. I pretty much lived in my imagination the whole time I was there. When I was released two years later, I started making things. It was the only way I could stay "present" and not slip back into my day dreams. To-day, the creatures in my thoughts still haunt me; I have to bring them to life or spend many sleepless nights obsessing over them. When I finish them all, I'll be free.

Dennis McNett

Before the end of the battle of Ragnorok, Hel saw how things were starting to unfold and retreated to the depths of the underworld. She managed to survive the fires that covered the earth the same way Odin's sons and the other Gods had dodged death. Here in the underworld, she has been planning the resurrection of her brothers and to reclaim their right to exist in the world.

Hel had already managed to find the remains of her brother Jörmungandr, the giant serpent, and had resurrected him along with several fallen warriors from her realm. After what had seemed like an eternity of searching, Hel recently found the remains of her other brother Fenris, the wolf giant. She has longed for this day because the resurrection of Fenris will assure the safety and strength needed to reenter the world without fear of being destroyed by the other Gods.

Allyson Mellberg

In my current works I am exploring the ways in which we communicate with each other and our environment (or fail to do so) and how that miscommunication manifests itself physically in our bodies and our surroundings. My characters exist in a void landscape where they desperately attempt to communicate with the people and animals around them. This work represents our efforts as humans, successful and unsuccessful, to empathize and interact with nature. In these works, animals seem dignified even though they are maimed and diseased; humans try in vain to care for animals in ways that make no sense. All of this is done with a sense of tenderness and humor mixed with the grotesque. The act of trying to nurture, care for, and grow something is important, even if it seems like unfamiliar territory.

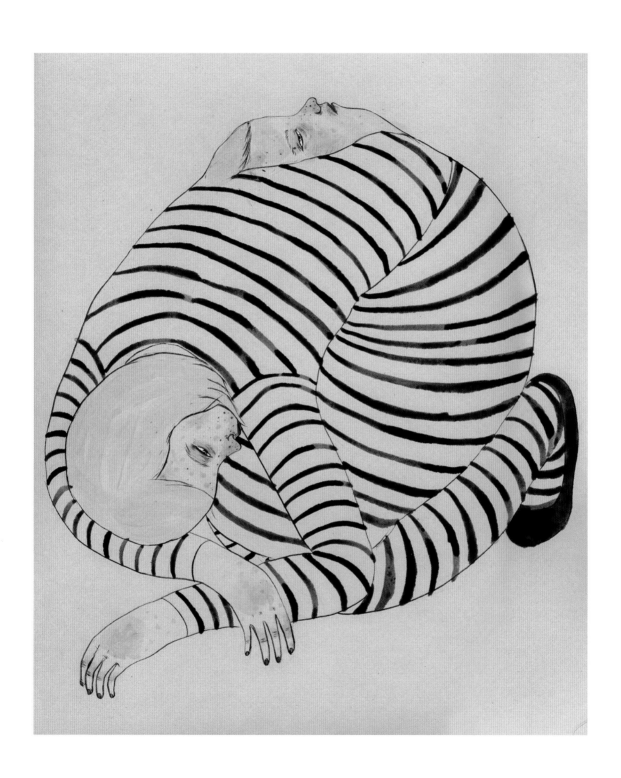

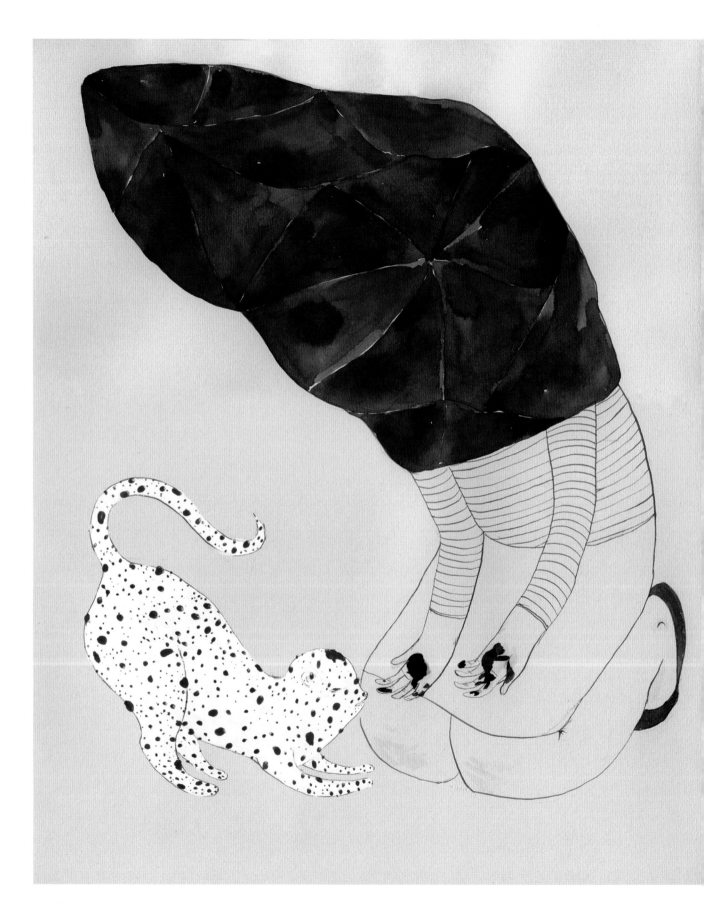

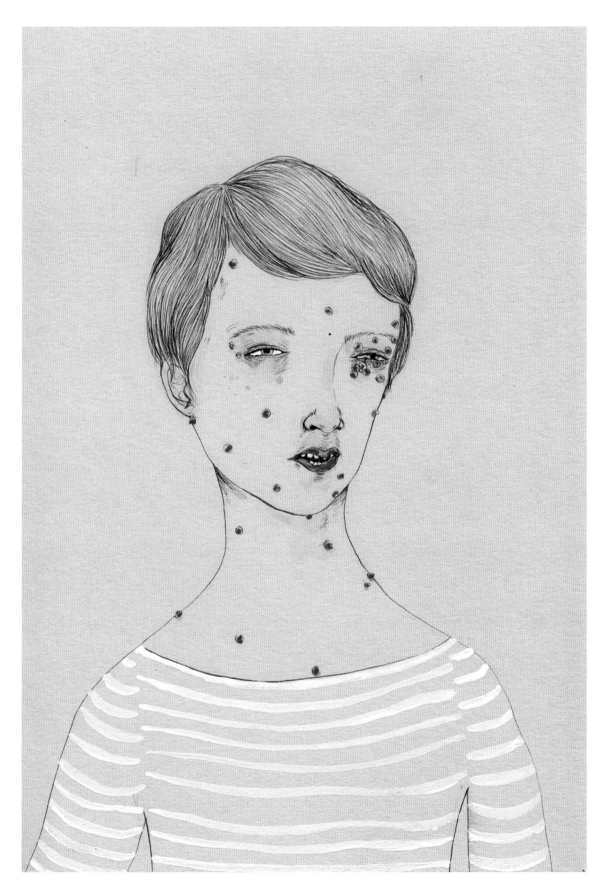

Miss Van

Dolores
Algernon Charles Swinburne

(Notre-Dame des Sept Douleurs)

Cold eyelids that hide like a jewel
Hard eyes that grow soft for an hour;
The heavy white limbs, and the cruel
Red mouth like a venomous flower;
When these are gone by with their glories,
What shall rest of thee then, what remain,
O mystic and sombre Dolores,
          Our Lady of Pain?

Polly Morgan

As a child, when it came to death, it was the decaying part I had difficulty with. I could accept the departure of the soul; after all, I'd seen plenty of things break and stop working. But in my house, they didn't always get thrown away; they would just be given a different purpose. If a bird no longer had use for its body then I'd have liked it as an ornament or inanimate pet, warm and soft in my pocket. Instead, I'd be told to find a matchbox or shoebox to bury the body in and would say goodbye for good.

Once while out shopping, my sister complained of a headache. My mother reached into her handbag to pull out an Anadin box. She proffered the open box, only to scream as a small hard hamster slid out onto my sister's palm. I must have picked up the wrong box and given some painkillers a funeral.

And here I am twenty years on, still fraternizing with the dead but in less upsetting ways I hope.

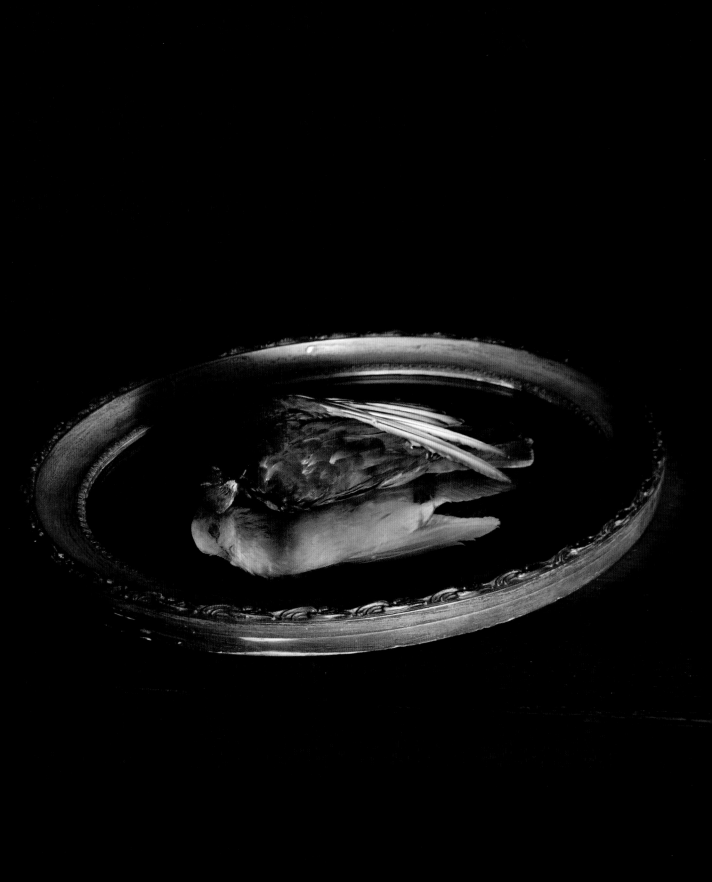

Munk One

I used to wake up with beads of sweat on my temples, heart racing, eyes darting around the room, just to make sure I was safe from the zombies in my nightmares. Thanks to growing up watching zombie movies as a kid, I would dream up amazingly long plot lines where I would run, fight and evade, but eventually be outnumbered with nowhere left to hide. What scared me most about those crazy dreams was that it was people I knew and loved who would turn on me when least expected. Much of my artwork blurs the thin line between what some would consider utterly horrific and that which is beautiful within the same form. A sort of balance seen throughout many aspects of life. I am fascinated by this duality, even as it rots and decays while chasing me down in my sleep...

Alex Pardee

As I was walking to my favorite deli where guessing the correct weight of a sandwich yields a prize, I saw a man get hit by a car. His hip slammed against the license plate on the car's raised bumper and the force of the impact caused half of his axial skeleton to instantly eject itself from the man's skin and muscles. The driver of the murder weapon didn't even slow down to apologize, or dare I say, laugh. I shouted uncontrollably and sprinted over to the victim but I quickly realized that he wasn't a man at all. What I watched explode onto the asphalt like a cartoon piñata, was actually just a plastic garbage bag with a few shreds of bone white paper and a cranberry juice box. Things like this happen to me all of the time. I guess my imagination takes over a lot and makes me see things that don't happen, and that don't exist. I try to draw and paint some of these experiences and creatures to share them with you, but I have a long way to go before I can really help you see what I see.

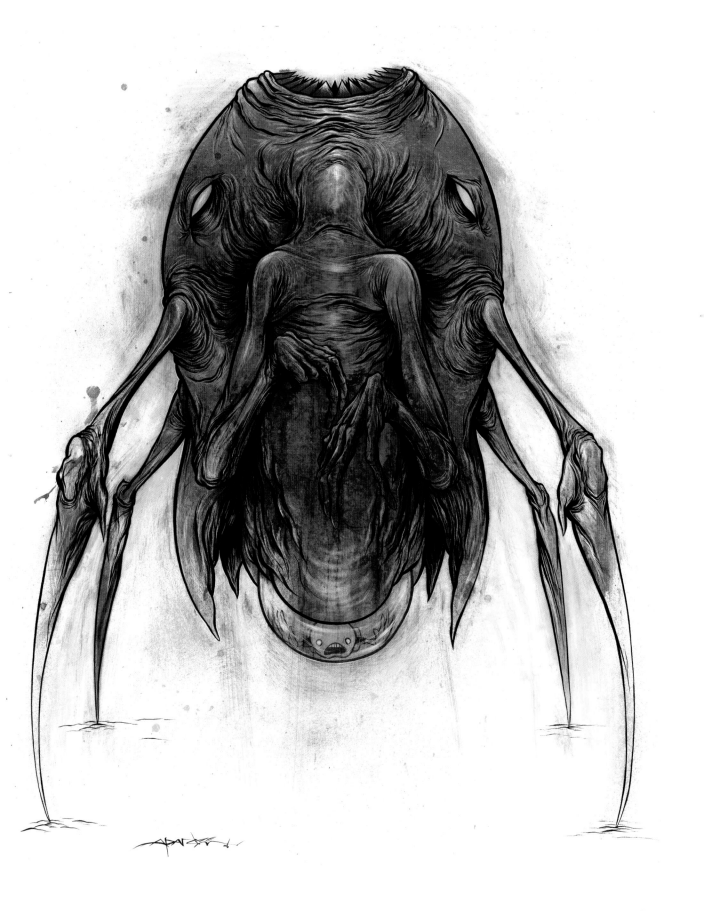

Cleon Peterson

I paint an anxiety-ridden dystopia where corruption and injustice plague the social order. Deviance prevails, as desperate characters struggle for power and control over their environment. The individual is displaced and forced to navigate this brutal world alone, finding hollow bits of pleasure and meaning in violence, sex, religion, and drugs. The crowd is an erratic mob-like authority bending outsiders to its will. It's a gray world where lawbreakers and law enforcers are one and the same: a world where ethics have been abandoned in favor of what every individual believes he's entitled to.

Suzanne
Sattler

This work stems from years of drawing conjoined twins and maimed figures. I was first interested in drawing their shapes and negative spaces - they were formally so beautifully unique to me. Over time their images led to questions on the dynamic of their relationships; their quality of life was completely dependent on how they chose to function together. How individuals relate to each other truly determines every aspect of their lives. I'm now interested in what shapes and forms these relationships, specifically the moments in which a successful balance is created. Every dynamic seen in our personal relationships can be explained more clearly through examples seen in nature, helping to explain these balances. Using a group of disfigured and feral subjects, I use these drawings to observe successful and failed attempts in various symbiotic relationships.

Greg 'Craola' Simkins

People often ask me, "Greg, how did you get the nickname Craola?" Well, it was in fourth grade and I was a tremendous pain in the neck to my teacher, so once again she locked me in the closet. It wasn't until the third hour that I heard a voice whisper to me, "I can get you out of here." To my surprise I whirled around and could just barely make out a shape in the dim light. As my eyes focused, I realized it was some kind of mouse spider. It was as if the top half of a mouse had been sewn to a spider's body. Can you believe that? And how could it talk? As it was explaining to me a way of escape, I could barely focus and grabbed the 64 pack of crayons off the shelf behind the abomination and squashed it with the box. Just then, my teacher opened the closet to see what the commotion was about and revealed the scene to the whole class. From then on I was known as Craola, the mouse/spider killer (but later dropped the end part). Oh yeah, I like to paint too. The end.

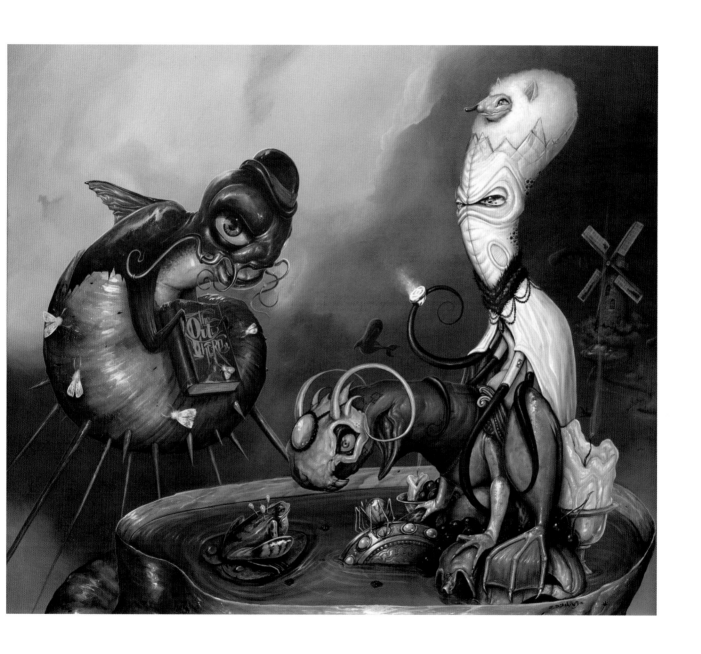

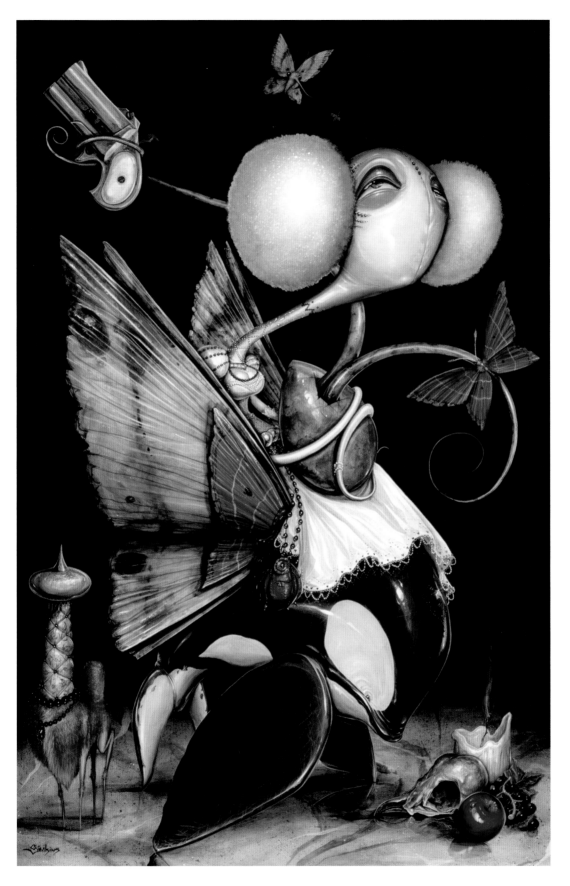

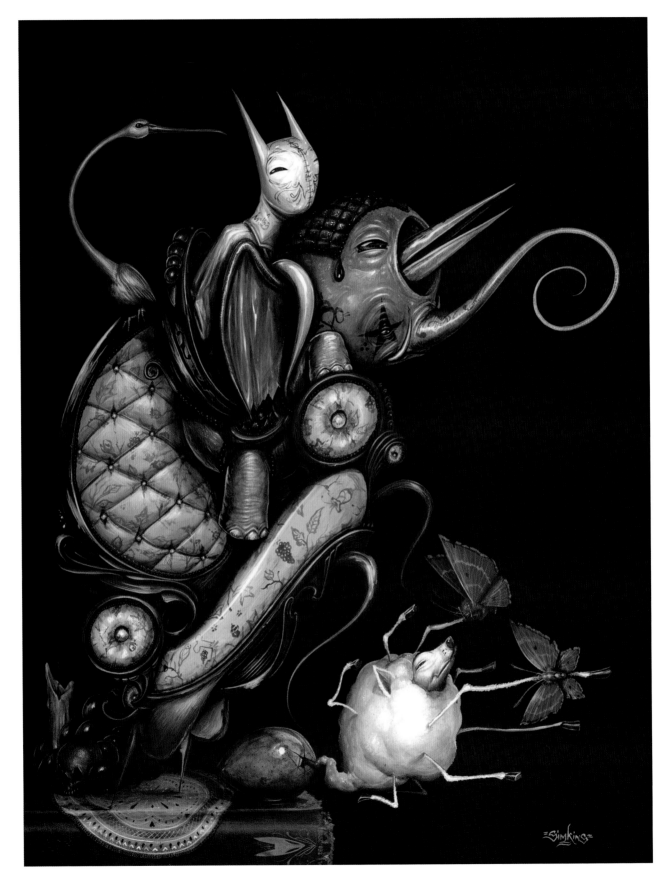

Skinner

I think it is spiritually harmful to eat meat in this day and time. There is no real act of connection in understanding the sacrifice an animal makes when its life is taken so that we may eat. I cannot draw a distinction between the values of two different creatures' lives. That is why I do not eat the animals of this planet. I don't feel like I would be given an adequate chance to show appreciation for its sacrifice before it was turned into a Happy Meal. Honoring sacrifice is a humble way of the past. Today, the cruel way that we treat our animals has turned on us in the forms of viruses and flus. I hope we pay as equally as the animals have for our convenience and that we all die painfully and in disgrace so that they may inherit the earth quietly and safely.

Jeff Soto

As a kid I lived in serious fear of a nuclear holocaust. We lived near March Air Force base and each night you could hear the nuclear weapon equipped B-52's taking off to fly north and meet up with Soviet TU-95's over Alaska. I found out later that these weren't B-52's, but unarmed refueling aircraft; had I known I think it still would have scared me awake each night. They were refueling the bombers that were already up there. This fear of war and nuclear armageddon was fueled by my imagination and a heavy dose of television - movies like *Red Dawn*, and *The Day After*, and cartoons like Thundarr the Barbarian and Robotech. I felt our future was inevitable. We were fucked. It was just a matter of time before raining fire would wipe out our species and the cockroach would emerge as the dominant earth inhabitant! I guess these thoughts still come out in my work from time to time...

Jonathan Viner

Before viewing Mr. Viner's work, please sign the following contract:

This agreement is made between Jonathan Viner of New York City, NY (hereinafter called the "Artist") and You, the Reader of Wherever You Live (hereinafter called the "Reader"). In consideration of the mutual promises and agreements of the parties hereto, as hereinafter set forth, it is agreed as follows:

1. The Reader agrees to follow the Artist's work and engage with the paintings to a degree equal to or greater than the engagement of the Artist to said marks on surfaces.
2. The Artist's transportation, housing, and meals, etc. are to be arranged and paid for by the Artist unless otherwise indicated.
3. In the event that either the Reader or the Artist is unable to fulfill its obligation due to damage or destruction of the Artist's imagery by fire, acts or regulations of public authorities, labor difficulties, civil tumult, strike, epidemic, and any unforeseen occurrence rendering the agreement impossible; neither the Artist nor the Reader shall be held legally responsible for any damages arising from cancellation of the agreement listed herein.

_____ (Artist Signature / Date)

_____ (Reader Signature / Date)

Marci Washington

I am interested in depicting a decadent society in the midst of crisis. I would like to tell a story set in a time that is both past and present - a carefully constructed collapse of historical time capable of revealing what is common between our society now and societies of the past. In this work I am focusing on the commonalities between our time and Edwardian England, the decadent height of British imperialism, a time of empire for the sake of empire, on the eve of World War I, and the beginning of the empire's decline.

I am building this story as if I am illustrating a novel that doesn't exist. If it did, it would probably be a lot like Wuthering Heights, Jane Eyre, or Bleak House - novels which use the popular conventions of fiction in order to seduce you into a story which ultimately functions as social commentary. I would like to highjack the ideological function of fiction - appropriating the character types and narrative conventions in order to construct an allegorical tale capable of challenging the simplistic cultural narrative of our own time in order to reveal a much darker tale of moral decline, spiritual crisis, and rampant anxiety.

ARTIST INDEX

WENDY COGAN-TOYODA
www.wendyct.com

HERBERT BAGLIONE
no site available

RICHARD COLMAN
www.richardcolmanart.com

IRANA DOUER
www.keepinmind.com.ar

STELIOS FAITAKIS
www.thebreedersystem.com

MATT FURIE
www.mattfurie.com

SEONNA HONG
www.seonnahong.com

JAMES JEAN
www.jamesjean.com

TRAVIS LOUIE
www.travislouie.com

CHRIS MARS
www.chrismarspublishing.com

ELIZABETH MCGRATH
www.lizmcgrath.com

DENNIS MCNETT
www.howlingprint.com

ALLYSON MELLBERG
www.cindersgallery.com

MISS VAN
www.missvan.com

POLLY MORGAN
www.pollymorgan.co.uk

MUNK ONE
www.munkone.com

ALEX PARDEE
www.eyesuckink.com

CLEON PETERSON
www.cleonpeterson.com

SUZANNE SATTLER
www.suzannesattler.com

GREG 'CRAOLA' SIMKINS
www.imscared.com

SKINNER
www.theartofskinner.com

JEFF SOTO
www.jeffsoto.com

JONATHAN VINER
www.vinerstudio.com

MARCI WASHINGTON
www.marciwashington.com

Image by: Richard Colman, Following Image by: Miss Van